Deliverance According to

JUDE

FAMILY ALTAR VERSION

EBENEZER GABRIELS
ABIGAIL EBENEZER-GABRIELS

19644 Club House Road Suite 815
Gaithersburg, Maryland 20886
www.EbenezerGabriels.Org
hello@ebenezergabriels.org

Ebenezer
Gabriels
ministries

TO

THE

LORD

GOD

WHO

DELIVERS

THE LORD OF HOSTS

Introduction to the book of

Jude

The written message is a crucial component of deliverance. JUDE, the writer of the letter, introduces himself as a "bond-servant" of Jesus. In the writings of Jude, you will find deliverance, restoration and the power of the Lord.

In this study, your family will learn the principles and rules of deliverance, you will learn that as God's called and chosen vessel you must remain open to the deliverance power of the Lord.

How to Use the Book of Jude Family Altar Deliverance Bible Study

There are 9 discussions

Each discussion is preceded by a Bible passage

Learn the Bible verse by heart - MEMORIZE

Each discussion has numbered segments

Read each segment each day

Discuss the knowledge from God's Word

Pray together with your loved ones

Bring your family together

Read the Scriptures

Read the discussion

Discuss the text

Featuring

Jude's 20 Principles of Deliverance

Prayer sets and discussions to bring your family together and usher your family into the deliverance of the Lord Jesus

Deliverance in the Book of Jude

9 Deliverance Discussions
Deliverance Highlights
Deliverance Prayer Sets to set your family altar ablaze

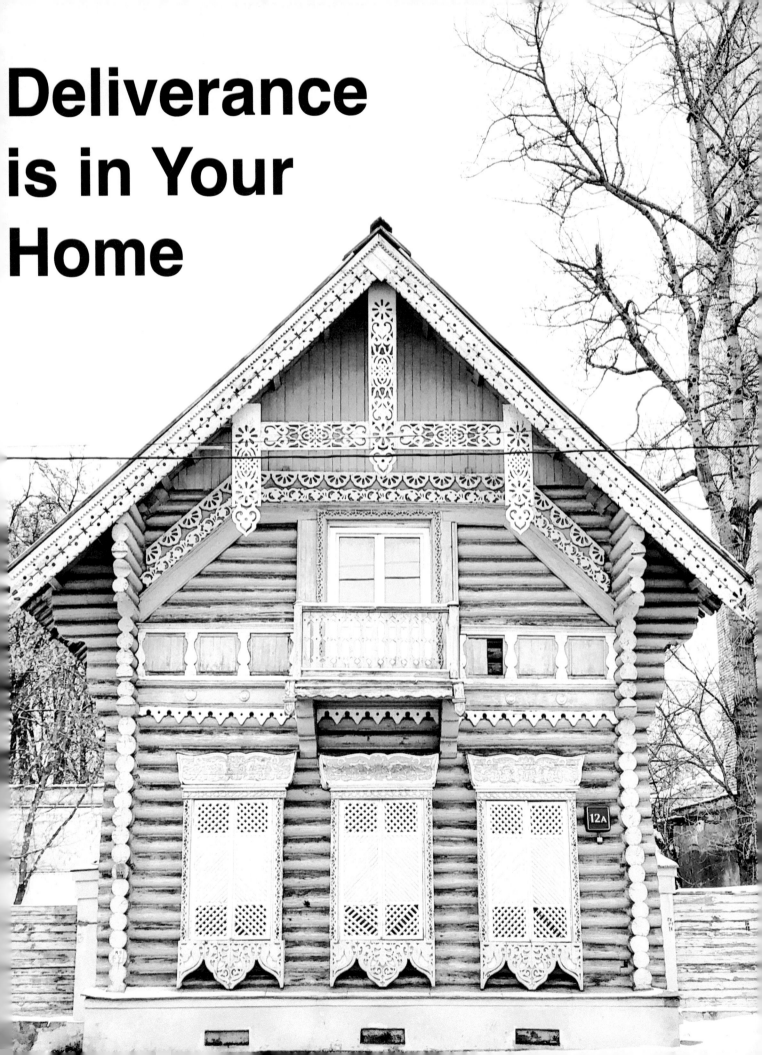

Deliverance is in Your Home

Discussion 1

The Book of Jude
Chapter 1 Verse 1

1
Jude,
a bondservant of Jesus Christ, and
brother of James,
To those who are called, sanctified
by God the Father, and preserved
in Jesus Christ

#1 Jude's Principle of Targeted Deliverance

The message of deliverance is targeted to a specific audience. Every family has a spiritual leader. Your family's spiritual leader is the custodian and facilitator of the deliverance message that the Lord has sent to your entire family.

This principle is found in Jude's opening address;

From: Jude

To: God's Anointed, God's Chosen, Carriers of God's Purpose, The Delivered, God's special People

Subject: A Message of Deliverance

Your Family is an Audience of God's Deliverance

The Principles of Targeted Deliverance in the book of Jude states that deliverance is for a targeted audience whether individuals, or families. Individuals and families are one of the major audiences of deliverance. Your family is a target of God's deliverance.

#2

Jude's Principle of Conceptualized Deliverance

Jude's introduction leads us into the concept of Bond Servanthood.

Who is a Bond-servant?

A bondservant - Someone whose heart is undetachable from serving and helping others. In Jude's situation, he introduces himself, describing his commitment as a loyal follower of Jesus. In the simple introduction of his letter, he also reminds the reader of his association with James.

In the family context, members of a family are bonded by love and blood.

Who is the "Called"?

The Called - Those who are beckoned to, and invited to the Father's special Presence. They are the elect carrying God's special purpose within them. The elect are leaders who are sent to bring others into deliverance.

In the family context, the "called" are those who are elected by the Lord's design to originate from a family line. In a church setting, the "called" are those who are ordained to be part of a local body of Christ per season. In any group or organization, the "called" are those who are ordained as part of a greater mission.

Deliverance Highlights - The Elect and the Uncalled

The uncalled lack the true bond of family

The elect who have been deceived manifest the orphan spirit by running away from home, or from their primary family purpose

The family bonded by the blood of Jesus is unbreakable

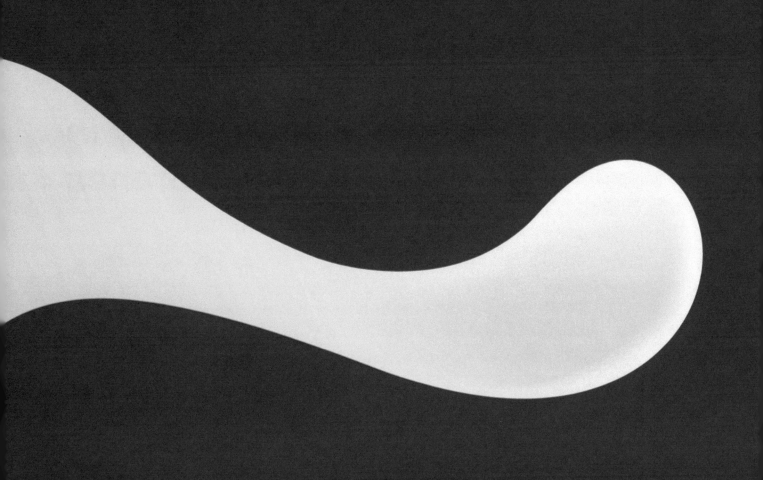

Deliverance Prayer Sets from the Book of Jude

ord, qualify us as your elect.
ord, Preserve us in Your will, in Jesus' Name.
Ve declare our allegiance to the Lord Jesus.
ord Jesus, bring our household into bond-servanthood with You.
ord Jesus, let all family members identify their true calling.
Dur family is bonded by the blood of Jesus.

Jude's Principle of Authority in Deliverance

Know your Master

Deliverance requires that you identify the master you serve - the Lord Jesus. Many families are under the captivity of the devil, in other words, Satan has become master over them and rules over their households. You must acknowledge the Lord as Savior and must have a tight-knitted relationship with the Lord Jesus, and use the authority from that relationship at all times, including when communicating.

Declare your Allegiance

The introduction to the book of Jude opens up with an insight that Jude's allegiance is to the Lord Jesus. His declaration of his allegiance to the Lord Jesus silences any threats or imagination seeking to question his spiritual authority.

Jude's message was directed to a unique audience - those who are called and loved. Those who have been called to fulfill a special assignment of the Lord, here on earth. Today, that would be leaders in all areas - leaders, families, community, government, church, marketplace industries.

It is a powerful undertaking to bring your entire family to declare allegiance to the Lord Jesus. The enemy will no longer have any foothold over any family member.

Jude's Deliverance Highlight

The message of deliverance is still very much relevant.
God sends the message of deliverance to His people.
Every message of deliverance has a purpose.
Every deliverance message is specific.

Deliverance Prayer Sets from the Book of Jude

Lord, qualify us as Your called.
Preserve us in Jesus.
We declare our allegiance to the Lord Jesus.
We are of Jesus, we know that and Jesus knows us as His.
Lord Jesus, bring Your targeted deliverance into our altar.
Lord, let the altar of our lives be ignited by Your fire.
Lord Jesus, strengthen the core of our family altar.
The Lord Jesus is the Master over our life's altar.
The Lord Jesus is the Master over our career altar.
The Lord Jesus is the Master over our marriage altar.
The allegiance of our family is to the Lord Jesus.
The allegiance of our household is to the Lord Jesus.

Discussion 2

The Book of Jude
Chapter 1 Verse 2

2
Mercy, peace, and love be multiplied
to you.

#4

Jude's Principle of Prayer-First in Deliverance

Prayer first in deliverance gives us the opportunity to function on higher realms, and conquered grounds, rather than having to go into war zones.

Open all Communication doors with Prayers: All types of communication doors, written or verbal, must be opened with prayers.

Prayer First: Praying brings us into the place of hiding in the name of Jesus, and benefitting from the finished works of Jesus Christ, so that we do not have to go into battle and leave Jesus behind.

While taking the prayer first approach, we are assured that the attention of the Lord is being brought into situations, and the help of heaven has been received.

Jude's Deliverance Highlights

God sends the message of deliverance to His people.
Every message of deliverance has a purpose
Families can imbibe the prayer-first minds by praying before eating or praying at the start of each day

Jude's Deliverance Prayer Sets

Lord Jesus, teach us the ways of Your deliverance.
Lord Jesus, give us the power of communication to hear from You.
Lord Jesus, overshadow us with the powe of prayers.
Lord Jesus, bring us into a higher realm prayers.
Lord Jesus, grow our household in praye and power.
Lord Jesus, bring our household into a place of faithfulness in prayers.

#5

Jude's Principle of Purposeful Prayers in Deliverance

Purposeful prayers are prayers targeted to help meet a specific purpose. There were three areas of requests as seen in Jude's prayer.

The Prayer for Mercy

He prayed for mercy. Mercy is needed when people are brought to the place of judgment, especially if they are deserving of condemnation. The power of God's mercy comes to deliver.

The Prayer for Love

In place of hate, Jude prays for the multiplication of love. Hateful prayers never amount to anything. Power and spirit-filled prayers are purposeful, and when deployed from the place of love, brings you great victory.

Purpose-filled Prayers

Purpose-filled prayers. Power and spirit-filled prayers are purposeful, and when deployed from the place of love, brings you great victory.

Purposeful prayers are led by the Holy Spirit. Flesh-inspired prayers are prayers prayed amiss, and are not purposeful, as it serves no purpose targeted to help meet a specific purpose.

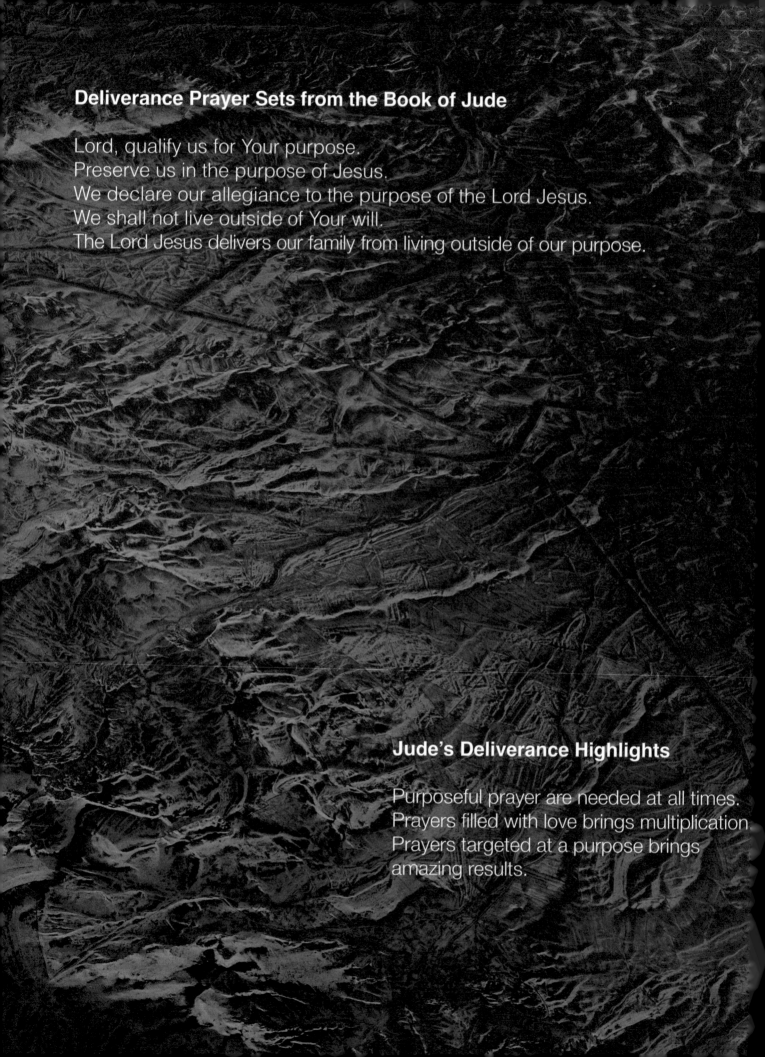

Deliverance Prayer Sets from the Book of Jude

Lord, qualify us for Your purpose.
Preserve us in the purpose of Jesus.
We declare our allegiance to the purpose of the Lord Jesus.
We shall not live outside of Your will.
The Lord Jesus delivers our family from living outside of our purpose.

Jude's Deliverance Highlights

Purposeful prayer are needed at all times.
Prayers filled with love brings multiplication
Prayers targeted at a purpose brings
amazing results.

Deliverance Prayer Sets for Families the Book of Jude

The Lord God of families, deliver our family by Your mercy.
The Lord God of families, deliver our family into purpose
The Lord God of families, deliver our family from obscurity by
Your love.
The Lord God of families, deliver our family from the raging
battles of loss of purpose.
The Lord God of families, deliver our family from loss in the
place of prayers.
Lord Jesus, deliver our family from lovelessness, in the name
of Jesus.

Discussion 3

The Book of Jude
Chapter 1 Verse 3-4

3

Beloved, while I was very diligent to write to you concerning our common salvation, I found it necessary to write to you exhorting you to contend earnestly for the faith which was once for all delivered to the saints.

4

For certain men have crept in unnoticed, who long ago were marked out for this condemnation, ungodly men, who turn the grace of our God into lewdness and deny the only Lord God and our Lord Jesus Christ..

#6

Jude's Principle of Diligence in Deliverance

Diligence is the deliverance leader's companion. The head of a family can be a deliverance leader, leading their family into deliverance. Jude exemplified diligence himself as he noted, "while I was very diligent" in his writing. He observed and understood through thoughts and considerations which are elements of diligence. He, then, found a strong reason to communicate with the leaders of deliverance.

Jude's Principles of Observation in Deliverance

Observation is one of the core principles of walking in God's deliverance. Jude observed an infiltration that was "unnoticed" and sounded the alarm, to call the attention of others in faith to a rising satanic and destructive trend which brings perversion.

For certain men have crept in unnoticed, who long ago were marked out for this condemnation, ungodly men, who turn the grace of our God into lewdness and deny the only Lord God and our Lord Jesus Christ.

Jude's Deliverance Highlights

Live diligently
Live in observation

Jude's Deliverance highlights

Lord Jesus, give us the gift of diligence.
Lord Jesus, multiply the gift of diligence upon our
household.
Lord Jesus, bring our household into the awareness of
who You are in the name of Jesus.
Lord Jesus, give us the gift of observation.

Discussion 4

Jude
Chapter 1 Verse 5-7

5
But I want to remind you, though you once knew this, that the Lord, having saved the people out of the land of Egypt, afterward destroyed those who did not believe.

6
And the angels who did not keep their proper domain, but left their own abode, He has reserved in everlasting chains under darkness for the judgment of the great day;

7
as Sodom and Gomorrah, and the cities around them in a similar manner to these, having given themselves over to sexual immorality and gone after strange flesh, are set forth as an example, suffering the vengeance of eternal fire.

#7

Jude's Principle of Faith in Deliverance

Faith is one of the founding principles of deliverance. Faithlessness brings hardship to deliverance. Believers must hold firm to God's voice which will scale them through hard times.

#8

Jude's Principles of Maintenance of Assigned Domain in Deliverance

Where is your primary place of assignment? Where has God sent your household?

Everyone, even angels have their assigned place. When found, we must learn to keep our proper domains. Slavery and captivity lie in wait for those who go outside their God-given authorized boundaries.

Individuals and families must understand their primary place of assignment to maintain the safety of God's Presence. You must avoid the temptation of being carried away by the calling of others which leads you out of your assigned domain.

#9

Jude's Principles of Abstinence from Communal Suffering in Deliverance

Everyone, even angels have the assigned place. When found, we mus learn to keep our proper domains Slavery and captivity lie in wait for thos who go outside their God-give authorized boundaries. Every part of th family must understand their role, an carry out their assignments accordin to their roles. Where there are rol exchanges, role abandonments households get into slavery. Where th husband refuses to rise and functio into his role, and the wife assumes h role, or where the wife does no function in her role and passes her ro to her husband or the children, th family enters into slavery.

Jude's Deliverance Highlights

The power of faith is limitless. There is power in staying in your assigned spaces. There is power in maintaining your boundaries in deliverance.

Jude's Deliverance Prayer Sets

Lord Jesus, give us the power to stay in our God given domain, in the name of Jesus. Lord Jesus, give us the understanding of boundaries in deliverance. Lord Jesus, cause a divine shift within our household, that You may align everyone into their right place and assignment. Lord Jesus, bring alignment into our household.

Discussion 5

Jude
Chapter 1 Verse 8-11

8

Likewise also these dreamers defile the flesh, reject authority, and speak evil of dignitaries.

9

Yet Michael the archangel, in contending with the devil, when he disputed about the body of Moses, dared not bring against him a reviling accusation, but said, "The Lord rebuke you!"

10

But these speak evil of whatever they do not know; and whatever they know naturally, like brute beasts, in these things they corrupt themselves.

11

Woe to them! For they have gone in the way of Cain, have run greedily in the error of Balaam for profit, and perished in the rebellion of Korah

#10

Jude's Principle of Honor in Deliverance

Honor is one of the gateways to deliverance. The rejection of authority and speaking falsely against authority is dishonorable, and the Lord frowns at it.

Where children reject parental authority, it becomes difficult to get into deliverance. Where the wife rejects the husband's authority, it becomes difficult to enter into deliverance as a family.Where the husband refuses to love or honor his wife, he rejects God's favor upon his life.

#11

Jude's Principles of God's Overruling in Deliverance

When deliverance leaders are faced with hard battles, and there is nowhere to turn, there are the warring angels calling for the Lord's rebuke upon the devil.

There is no place for pride in deliverance, but there is always the name of the Lord to run into when help is needed.

#12

Jude's Principles of Staying Steadfast in God in Deliverance

There are ways that displeases the Lord, these are the ways of Cain whose sacrifice was not accepted, and those who work in greed. Greed brings error, and also rebellion. All these the Lord hates.

In deliverance, God's people are to depart from the ways of rebellion, greed and ungratefulness, as these are major blockers of deliverance.

Jude's Deliverance Highlights

The power of staying out of the pits of greed and rebellion.
The power in submission to parental or spousal authority.

Jude's Deliverance Prayer Sets

Lord Jesus, visit our household with Your honor.
Lord Jesus, give us a heart that is steady.
Lord Jesus, cast away all spirits of dishonor at work in our family.
Lord Jesus, cast away all attitude of dishonor from our family.
Lord Jesus, cast away all behavior of rebellion from our family in
the name of Jesus.

Discussion 6

Jude
Chapter 1 Verse 12-15

12
These are spots in your love feasts, while they feast with you without fear, serving only themselves. They are clouds without water, carried about by the winds; late autumn trees without fruit, twice dead, pulled up by the roots;

13
raging waves of the sea, foaming up their own shame; wandering stars for whom is reserved the blackness of darkness forever.

14
Now Enoch, the seventh from Adam, prophesied about these men also, saying, "Behold, the Lord comes with ten thousands of His saints,

15
to execute judgment on all, to convict all who are ungodly among them of all their ungodly deeds which they have committed in an ungodly way, and of all the harsh things which ungodly sinners have spoken against Him

Jude's Principle of Staying Grounded in Deliverance

#13

Substance is power in the place of deliverance. The lack of it is called emptiness. Clouds without rain display arrogance without something of Godly worth to back up arrogant claims.

God's children are called to a life of power, and the demonstration of God's power, living a life worthy of the calling Jesus has called forth.

Families are called to have substance. Families are not called to go back and forth in unsteadiness. Family life is supposed to bring stability.

Jude's Principles of Godly Judgment in Deliverance

#14

God brings justice across all forms of injustices at the right time. Pride brings shame, wandering, ungodliness invites the wrath of God.

Substance is power in the place of deliverance. Where there is unending sin, judgment comes. God's children must not usurp God's grace because there is an end to that too.

Jude's Deliverance Highlights

The power of humility.
The power of deliverance.

Jude's Deliverance Prayer Sets

Lord Jesus, bring us into the place of steadiness in deliverance.
Lord Jesus, judge in our favor for our deliverance.
Lord Jesus, let not our family be a usurper of Your grace.
Lord Jesus, wipe away shame from our household.
Lord Jesus, break the yoke of ungodliness from off our necks.

Discussion 7

Jude
Chapter 1 Verse 16-19

16
These people are grumblers and faultfinders; they follow their own evil desires; they boast about themselves and flatter others for their own advantage.

17
But, dear friends, remember what the apostles of our Lord Jesus Christ foretold.

18
They said to you, "In the last times there will be scoffers who will follow their own ungodly desires."

19
These are the people who divide you, who follow mere natural instincts and do not have the Spirit.

Jude's Principle of Alertness and Positivity in Deliverance

Tools of Satan to deceive God's children include: complain, lust, and sometimes flatter. God's children must stay alert, and filled with the Holy Spirit to wade off the enemy's resources.

The Apostles forewarned believers about this; this satanic practice continues to exist till date. How can believers handle this?

Alertness is the state of being aware and present. Staying alert ensures that you do not get lost, in spiritual battles, or the physical.

Grumbling and complaining is a spirit that accompanies the lack of gratitude. It is an anti-worship spirit that seeks to point fingers. This spirit also brings accusation, and you must learn to conquer this power.

Jude's Deliverance Highlights

Stay alert in your mind that the spirit of complaints will not overshadow you.
Get away from all appearances of evil and lustful desires.
Understand the workings of the spirit of grumbling and complaining and nab
it before it starts.

Jude's Deliverance Prayer Sets

Lord Jesus, fill us with the power to overcome the spirit of lust
Lord Jesus, fill us with the power to overcome the spirit of complaints.
Lord Jesus, fill our family up with the power of awareness.
Lord Jesus, cast out the spirit of complaining and grumbling out of our
family.

Discussion 8

The Book of Jude
Chapter 1 Verse 20-22

20
But you, beloved, building yourselves up on your most holy faith, praying in the Holy Spirit,

21
keep yourselves in the love of God, looking for the mercy of our Lord Jesus Christ unto eternal life.

22
And on some have compassion, making a distinction;

23
but others save with fear, pulling them out of the fire, hating even the garment defiled by the flesh.

Jude's Principle of Tongue-Speaking in Deliverance #16

Speaking in tongues has been an object of dissension in many groups. However the book of Jude advises that believers who are elect should pray in the tongues as it helps grow your spiritual stature.

It is a beautiful and powerful act when a family prays in the Holy Spirit. This gift is released when you ask the Lord for it.

#17 Jude's Principles of Delivering others in Deliverance

We are called to deliver others too, however possible. Every believer has been called to preach the message of salvation to the unsaved. This is such an urgent Word that requires that we snatch the unsaved out of the way of perdition. In families, pray the prayers of deliverance for your household.

#18 Jude's Principles of Love in Deliverance

Love remains the currency of connecting with the Lord in deliverance. Through love, the greatest battle can be won. Every family approaching deliverance must learn to preserve the love of God in their lives. When a family is not bonded in love, it's hard to win battles.

Jude's Deliverance Highlights

Speak in tongues, it's a second nature to deliverance.
Encourage family members to pray for the gift of tongues.
Love the Lord, and continue loving on Him, this is the only hope.
Pray for other family members.
Pray for the deliverance of all family members
Show love to others too.

Jude's Deliverance Prayer Sets

Lord, open our tongue into the deeper realm of your power.
Lord Jesus, display Your love over our lives.
Lord Jesus, bless our household with the spirit of tongues.
Lord Jesus, we pray for deliverance of our household from communal slavery in the name of Jesus.
Lord Jesus, we pray for deliverance of our household from communal affliction in the name of Jesus.

Discussion 9

The Book of Jude
Chapter **1** Verse **20-22**

24
Now to Him who is able to keep you
from stumbling, And to present you
faultless
Before the presence of His glory
with exceeding joy,

25
To God our Savior,
Who alone is wise,
Be glory and majesty,
Dominion and power,
Both now and forever.
Amen.
.

Jude's Principle of Purity in Deliverance #19

The Lord seeks to wash us clean and purify us. God's people must be open to the cleansing and sanctification of the Lord, as the goal of this is to present you back to the Lord.

A home filled with God's purity will usher in God's deliverance. Purity comes from continually hearing the Word of God. When sin consumes a family, there is no purity. When the spirit of sin dwells in the family, sin is passed from one person to the other. In a family living under the atmosphere of sin, there's incest, underaged sex, sexual abuse and all sorts of abomination that ruins the land of the family.

#20 Jude's Principles of Worship in Deliverance

Worship has always been a part of deliverance - it's inseparable. Worship is a natural response for deliverance, it is powerful, and the Lord yields to the voice of worship. Worshippers must get into the habit of extolling the name of the Lord - this brings major deliverance.

When the family worships the Lord, the Lord's altar is cultivated upon the family, and the enemy is cast out.

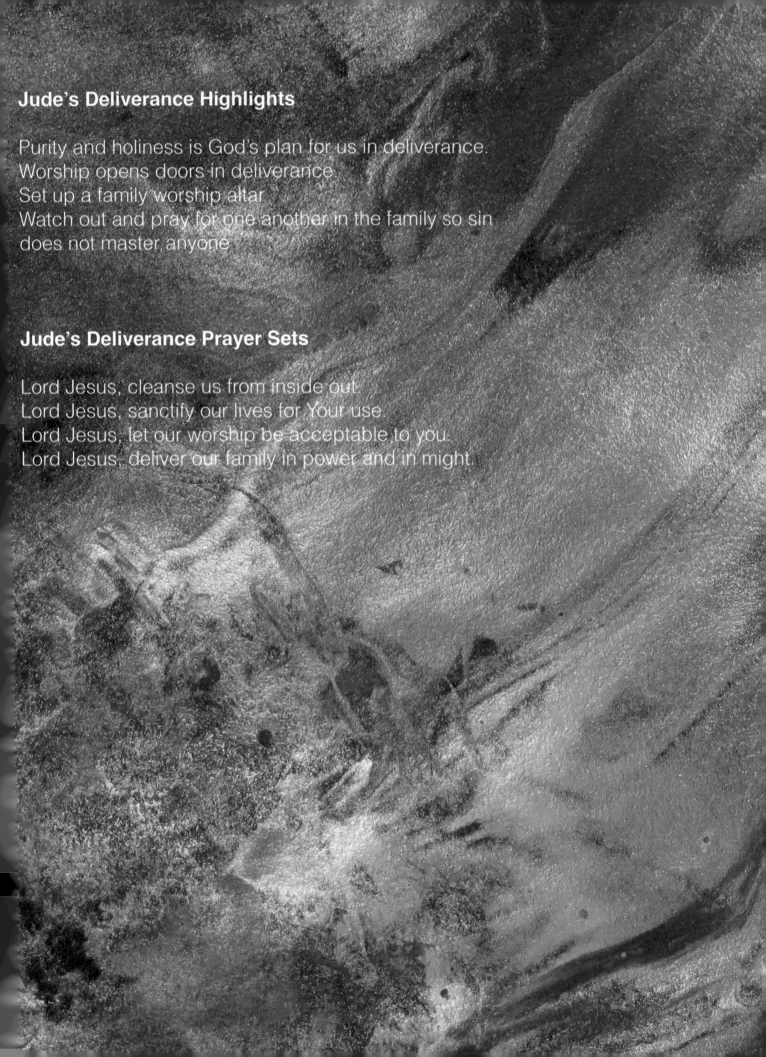

Jude's Deliverance Highlights

Purity and holiness is God's plan for us in deliverance.
Worship opens doors in deliverance.
Set up a family worship altar
Watch out and pray for one another in the family so sin
does not master anyone

Jude's Deliverance Prayer Sets

Lord Jesus, cleanse us from inside out.
Lord Jesus, sanctify our lives for Your use.
Lord Jesus, let our worship be acceptable to you.
Lord Jesus, deliver our family in power and in might.

RAISING

A

PROPHETIC

AND

CURSE-FREE

GENERATION

EXPLORE OUR COMMUNITIES

Subscribe to TV, Bible Study and Devotional Plans at

www.iamuncursed.com

IAUC
Bible School and
Ministry Certifications

The IAUC School of Ministry is one of the five schools under the Ebenezer Gabriels Schools of the Holy Spirit. The IAUC offers

Prophetic Ministry Certificate Program, Deliverance Ministry Certificate Program and Prophetic Worship Certificate Program

Marriage Education and Retreats & Singles Education

Enroll in the Marriage Preparation or Marriage Deliverance and Singles Programs

About I am Uncursed - IAUC

A Biblical Deliverance, Deliverance Education and Platform

The deliverance of Jesus is here. Uncursed has grown from a stack of prayer pages carried around in a folder, to the Uncursed book available in multi-languages and to the I am Uncursed community, a deliverance and curse-breaking platform.

At iamuncursed.com, we are sharing God's Word of deliverance and of power in dynamic ways; through deliverance devotionals, exploration of on-demand deliverance topics and most importantly, Bible study on deliverance. Uncursed is the platform for deliverance discipleship. Ministers of deliverance and seekers of deliverance are getting delivered now, and being equipped for the next season in their lives.

The deliverance ministry is needed across; there are only a few vessels who have obtained the authority to minister deliverance. God is planting His Word into the souls of His people, that they may learn deliverance from His Word and through the teachings of anointed leaders.

INCLUYE

Oraciones de Sanidad Interna

Oraciones de Liberación Generacional

Oraciones de Liberación Regresando al
Vientre

Oraciones Durante el Embarazo

Ebenezer Gabriels
Abigail Gabriels

Second
Edition

FEATURES

Inner Healing Prayers

Foundational Deliverance Prayers

Back-to-the Womb Deliverance Prayers

Pregnancy Season Prayers

Ebenezer Gabriels
Abigail Gabriels

The Uncursed Book

Biblical and Prophetic Foundational
Deliverance Book to Raise a curse-less
Generation. We invite you to go on a
deliverance retreat with your family
while you engage in the acts of
foundation warfare for the setting free of
your entire family lineage using the
revelations of the Holy Spirit in the
Uncursed Book as a resource and the
Scripture as a guide.

UNCURSED

A PROPHETIC BOOK TO RAISE A CURSELESS GENERATION

Second
Edition

FEATURES

Inner Healing Prayers

Foundational Deliverance Prayers

Back-to-the Womb Deliverance Prayers

Pregnancy Season Prayers

Ebenezer Gabriels
Abigail Gabriels

SIN MALDICIÓN

Ebenezer Gabriels

Ebenezer Gabriels

About the Authors

Ebenezer Gabriels is a Worshiper, Innovation Leader, Prophetic Intercessor, and a Computer Scientist who has brought heaven's solutions into Financial markets, Technology, Government with his computational gifts. Prophet Gabriels is anointed as a Prophetic Leader of nations with the mantle of healing, worship music, national deliverance, foundational deliverance, complex problem-solving and building Yahweh's worship altars.

Abigail Ebenezer-Gabriels is Pastor, Teacher, Worshiper and a Multi-disciplinary leader in Business, Technology, Education and Development. She is blessed with prophetic teaching abilities with the anointing to unveil the mysteries in the Word of God. She is a Multi-specialty Speaker, with a special anointing to explain Heaven's ordinances on earth.

Both Ebenezer Gabriels and Abigail Ebenezer-Gabriels are the founders of the Ebenezer Gabriels Schools of the Holy Spirit and are the Senior Pastors of LightHill Church Gaithersburg, Maryland.

They lead several worship communities including the 6-Hour Worship unto Deliverance, Innovation Lab Worship encounters, Move this Cloud - and prophetic podcast communities including the Daily Prophetic Insights and Prophetic Fire where God's agenda for each day is announced and the manifold wisdom of God is revealed on earth. Both Ebenezer Gabriels and his wife, Abigail Ebenezer-Gabriels joyfully serve the Lord through lifestyles of worship and their mandate is to build worship altars to intercede for nations.

About Ebenezer Gabriels Ministries

At Ebenezer Gabriels Ministries (EGM), we fulfill the mandate of building worship altars by sharing the story of the most expensive worship ever offered by Jesus Christ, the Son of God and dispersing the aroma of the knowledge of Jesus Christ to the ends of the world.

Ebenezer Gabriels Publishing delivers biblically grounded learning experiences that prepare audiences for launch into their prophetic calling. We create educational contents and deliver in innovative ways through online classrooms, apps, audio, prints to enhance the experience of each audience as they are filled with the aroma of Christ knowledge and thrive in their worship journey. EGM currently operates out of Gaithersburg in Maryland, USA.

Contact

Mailing
19644 Club House Road Suite 815,
Gaithersburg, Maryland, 20876 USA

iamuncursed.com
hello@ebenezergabriels.org
www.ebenezergabriels.org

Other Books by

Ebenezer Gabriels
&
Abigail Gabriels

Mind

Deliverance from the Yokes Deep Mysteries of Creation in the Realms of Thoughts, Imaginations and Words

Spiritual War and Prayers

Rapid Fire

The Big Process called Yoke

Deliverance of the Snares of the Fowler

The only Fire that Extinguishes Witchcraft

No longer Fugitives of the Earth

Subduers of the Earth

Prayers of the Decade

Growth and Advancing in Faith

Deeper Mysteries of the Soul (English, Spanish, Arabic and Chinese)

Men: Called out of the Dunghill

Women: Bearers of Faith

New Beginnings in Christ

Wisdom my Companion

Deeper Mysteries of the Blood

Explore the Ebenezer-Gabriels Communities

Become a part of our communities

Deliverance and Prophetic Community: www.iamuncursed.com

Marriage Community: www.blissfulmarriageuniversity.com

Singles Community: compass.blissfulmarriageuniversity.com

Children's Learning Community: www.inspiremylittleone.com

Business Leadership Programs: www.unprofanedpurpose.com

Ebenezer Gabriels Prophetic Evangelistic Ministries: www.ebenezergabriels.org